The waves . . .

CR-A-A-A-A-SH

in.

And then . . .

cr-e-e-e-p

out.

Swish, *gurgle, trickle,*
drip-drip-drop.

Seawater collects
between the rocks.
And quiet settles
over the shore.

And . . .

For K.B. —C.F.

Thanks to Felicia, Sarah, and all my friends at the Pacific Science Center for providing inspiration for this book —A.H.

Neal Porter Books

Library of Congress Cataloging-in-Publication Data

Names: Fleming, Candace, author. | Hevron, Amy, illustrator.
Title: The tide pool waits / written by Candace Fleming ; illustrated by
    Amy Hevron.
Description: First edition. | New York : Holiday House, [2022] | "A Neal
    Porter Book." | Includes bibliographical references. | Audience: Ages 4
    to 8 | Audience: Grades K–1 | Summary: "A lyrical tour of the ecology of
    tide pools"— Provided by publisher.
Identifiers: LCCN 2021005547 | ISBN 9780823449156 (hardcover)
Subjects: LCSH: Tide pool ecology—Juvenile literature. | Tide
    pools—Juvenile literature.
Classification: LCC QH541.5.S35 F54 2022 | DDC 577.69/9—dc23
LC record available at https://lccn.loc.gov/2021005547

ISBN: 978-0-8234-4915-6 (hardcover)

The Tide Pool Waits

Candace Fleming

Pictures by

Amy Hevron

NEAL PORTER BOOKS

HOLIDAY HOUSE / NEW YORK

The sun rises
and brightens the sky.

It dries the sand.
It dries the rocks.
It heats the trapped seawater.
Warmer.

And warmer.
And warmer still.

"*Keow-keow!*" cries a gull.
It circles down to spread its
wings in the morning light.

At pool's edge, clusters of barnacles
shut out the day's heat.
Beds of mussels close up tight, too.
So do turban snails.
And limpets.
And chitons.

They wait.

At pool's bottom,
baby opaleyes school together.
Suspended.
Motionless.
Blending in.

They wait.

The octopus slips into a crack.
The sea star grips a craggy shelf.

The sculpin hides
behind the algae.

They wait.

There are others, too.

Under rocks.

In the tangle of floating, fanning seaweed.

Beneath the sand and between patches of sponge.

They all wait.

And wait.

And wait.

The restless ocean waits, too,
for the earth and the moon,
the sun and the wind,

for just the right time to . . .

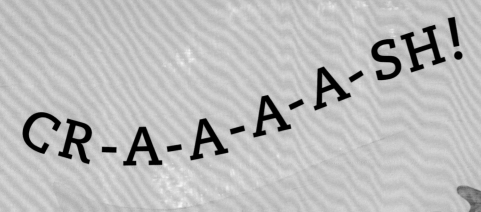

CR-A-A-A-SH!

Waves,

    wild and roaring,

cold and foaming,

      sweep toward shore.

They surge over barnacles, mussels, and snails,
stir the tangle of seaweed,
shake the crevice-cracked rocks,

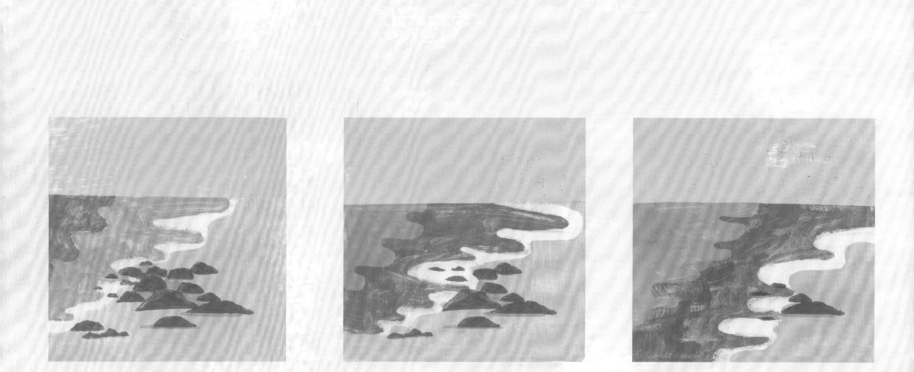

rise higher and higher and higher until . . .

the pool is part
of the sea once more.

The tide has come.
The wait is over.

Sea anemones bloom on the rocks.
Shrimp paddle out of the seaweed.
Tubeworms poke from the sand
while sea slugs slither across sponge.

The barnacles open their shells and sweep in food with their feathery feet. Time to eat.

The sea star creeps across the rocks. Time to hunt.

The octopus glides to the surface.
Time to return to the open sea.

As the octopus
swims out,
a periwinkle washes in.
It swirls down
into a bed of rockweed.

Out sidles a kelp crab, touching, exploring.

Out scoots a rock crab,
searching, scavenging.

Time to fight?

Not today.

Opaleyes flash and dart.
Sea urchins wave.

Shannies play hide-and-seek in the seaweed.

Sea squirts shoot water from their tubes.

Scallops *clap-clap* their shells.

A sea cucumber inches across the sand.

The sculpin opens its mouth and waits
for a meal.

Everything is busy.
All brim with life.

But the sea can't resist
the pull of the moon,
the turn of the earth,
the sun and the wind.

Swish, *gurgle, trickle,*
drip-drip-drop.

Once again, the waves

cr-e-e-e-e-p

out.

And seawater collects between the rocks.
And quiet settles over the shore.

And . . .

the tide pool waits.

An Illustrated Guide to This Tide Pool

Twice a day when the tide goes out—called low tide—an astonishing world is revealed in the tide pools that form along the Pacific Coast. Some of the creatures that live there look like stone. Others look like plants. Some move so slow it's hard to tell if they're actually moving, while others are so fast you're not sure you really saw them. The biggest animals in the pool are smaller than your hand, while the smallest can't be seen without a microscope. During low tide, all these creatures—big, slow, fast, small—are exposed to air and the sun's drying heat. And so they have developed ways to survive the wait until ocean's return—high tide. Let's take a closer look at some of these animals:

Don't let these **barnacles** fool you. They aren't rocks but soft, slimy creatures that live inside shells. During high tide, barnacles open up their shells, wave their legs, and grab bits of food floating by. When the tide starts to go out, barnacles click their shells shut while they're full of water. This keeps the animal moist while it waits for high tide's return.

Mussels also live inside two shells squeezed tightly together to hold in moisture and keep out predators. At high tide, they open up and filter food through their gills. Mussels gather in "beds," gluing themselves to rocks, and even one another, with thick threads made from special secretions. So tough are mussels that they can withstand up to twenty years of crashing, pounding waves.

Crabs, like kelp and rock crabs, are the cleanup crew of the tide pool. They will eat anything they can find—dead plants, animals, algae. Their big front claws, called pincers, are used for digging and fighting. If one falls off, a new pincer grows back. The small, strong kelp crab can be hard to spot because it perfectly matches the algae it lives in. The rock crab, meanwhile, buries itself in the sand to camouflage its brick-red shell.

Green, orange, pink, tan, and lavender—**anemones** may look like flowers, but they are really animals. Clinging to rocks with an adhesive foot, they "bloom" during high tide by extending their stinging tentacles to sweep plankton and small fish into their mouths. When the water ebbs, they pull in their tentacles and wait for the waves to return.

It's easy to see where the **sea cucumber** got its name. But even though they're shaped like the garden vegetable and don't have faces (or even any eyes), they are animals. Slow moving and shy, sea cucumbers stay on the tide-pool floor, usually between rocks, where they suck up tiny particles of algae and microscopic marine animals. If attacked, some species will shoot out sticky threads that snare and confuse their predators. Others will spit out their innards, giving the predator something to eat while they scoot away on their five rows of tube feet. Once safe, they grow back their internal organs.

Periwinkles and **turban snails** love to munch on algae. At low tide, these snails creep along scraping algae off rocks with their raspy tongues. When the tide goes out, they use their single foot to tightly grip the rocks so as not to be washed out to sea by crashing waves. Their curled shells protect them from predators like sea stars and crabs. As they grow, they add to their shell so they are always safe inside a house that fits their bodies.

Limpets and **chitons** live under their shells on rocks like tiny, upside-down saucers. With their one, large foot, they can cling unmoving to surfaces even when waves pound. Both scrape rock until they've made a tiny hollow that perfectly fits their shells. This "home scar" traps water to help them stay moist during low tide. Both creatures forage short distances in search of algae. But they always leave a mucus trail so they can find their way home.

Small fish, like **opaleyes** and **shannies**, live in the tide pools until they are big enough to live in deep water. **Sculpins**, however, are especially made for life in the tide pool. Incredibly, sculpins can breathe air and even survive out of water for a few hours if kept moist. They have bulging eyes atop their head so they can see what might be coming from above, like a hungry gull or octopus. They also have a keen sense of smell. If a sculpin is washed out of its favorite tide pool by the waves, it can find its way back by following the scent trail.

Sponges are simple animals. They cannot move or respond to their environment. Instead of mouths, they have tiny pores that suck in seaweed and then strain out the particles of foods. Most sponges grow on rocks or in crevices.

Sometimes a young **octopus** will get swept into a tide pool by high tide. Stuck when the water recedes, this smart, eight-armed creature will hide until high tide returns by slipping into a crevice or changing color to blend into its surroundings. It might even have a snack while it waits. Watch out, crabs and sea urchins!

A tide pool is the perfect nursery for baby **shrimp**. Safely hidden in the algae, they munch on plant matter and dead fish until they're big enough (five to eight inches) for the deep ocean.

What animal has eyes on the tips of its arms and its mouth on its underside? A **sea star**, of course! It camps out near the base of rocks or under a mussel bed during low tide to stay moist. When the tide comes in, it uses its sucker-tipped tube feet to climb up and hunker down on top of its prey—usually a mussel or limpet. It will pull on the shells for hours, trying to pry them open and get to the creature inside. Sometimes low tide forces the sea star to give up. Other times, the sea star manages to crack open a shell. Then it pushes its stomach out of its mouth and between the shells to slurp up its meal. Yum!

Sea urchins have sharp spines and nipping pincers to defend themselves from crabs, anemones, and fish that find them delicious. They also have tube feet to help them glide along rocky surfaces. A special set of jaws with five sharp teeth help scrape its algae lunch off rocks or take bites out of its favorite food: giant kelp. These same jaws help it dig out a cubbyhole in soft rock that not only gives it a place to hide but also fills with water before low tide, helping to keep the urchin moist.

Sea squirts begin life by swimming, tadpole-like, around the tide pool. After finding a good spot to settle, they cement their head to the spot so they can never leave. Then they absorb their tails, and their gills turn into siphons—one to draw in water and filter out food (plankton), the other to expel waste. They're called sea squirts because when scared, they shoot water from both siphons.

Let's Explore

You can explore tide pools even if you don't live near the coast. Here are a few sites to get you started:

The best site on Pacific Coast tide pools is hosted by Kasey Eunice and other marine biologists who take you right into tide pools. Each video episode found on the site lets you meet, up close, the creatures who call this environment their home—mussels and clams, sea slugs and nudibranches, crabs and lobsters . . . and more! Don't forget to take the fun quiz after you've seen it all. www.lifeinatidepool.com

Visitors to the Seacoast Science Center's Virtual Tide Pool can click and explore a teeming tide pool. Don't forget to look under the rocks. prezi.com/view/Xfl9XHaKnu6TkWti6jsf/

Walk the low tide at Point Lobos State Natural Reserve in California alongside a scientist from the Monterey Bay Aquarium and a California State Park officer as they race against the incoming tide in search of curious and amazing creatures. www.youtube.com/watch?v=wpySMliPqNc

We are deeply indebted to Dr. Jayson Smith, PhD, Professor of Biology at California State Polytechnic University, Pomona, for sharing his time, knowledge, and passion for Pacific Coast tide pools, as well as for meticulously fact-checking both the text and the illustrations found in this book. Big thanks also to the aquarists at the Shedd Aquarium in Chicago for setting up a behind-the-scenes walk-through of the Pacific Coast tide-pool habitat in the Abbott Oceanarium.

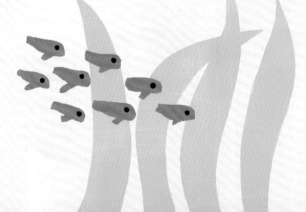

Where Do They Live?

The spray zone is dampened by ocean spray and waves but is almost never covered by water.

limpets

periwinkles

The high tide zone stays dry for long stretches. It is covered in water only at the peak of high tide. This zone takes a lot of pounding from the waves.

barnacles

shore crabs such as hermit crabs

mussels

The middle tide zone has more animals living in it than the previous two because the tide ebbs and flows over it twice a day. During low tide, it will be exposed. At high tide, it will be covered by water.

sea stars

sea anemones

chiton

limpet

sea slug

sponge

The low tide zone is almost always under water. When the tide is out, the water grows warmer and saltier until, at last, high tide brings refreshment.

octopus

fish

sea urchins

rock crab

algae

sea cucumber

kelp crab